"For those readers, men and women, who wish to enrich their love lives, investigating Catherine's sage and well-considered advice could be just the answer and the path you're looking for!"

— *Osho Times*, international online magazine

"For many years there have been books about how to be tricky, guarded, or false in the world of dating by "the rules." Thank goodness that Catherine Auman has spelled out a different and better way. This is a book for people who want integrity, authenticity, and genuine connection to truly happen. It's a much-needed approach that feels both new and timeless."

— Leonard Felder, PhD, author of *Fitting in is Overrated*

"I love this book. Thank you, Catherine Auman. If you haven't read or don't know anything about the tantric approach to dating, check out this book and consider attending one of Catherine's workshops—truly game changing."

— Carina Eriksson, Professional Matchmaker

"The book *Tantric Dating* offers much-needed clarity and insight into the world of sacred sexuality and the much-bantered term "tantra". The author is the real deal and she teaches that love is always available and changing our perception is an important place to begin."

— Corey Folsom, Sex & Relationship Coach

"When it comes to dating coaching, I would completely trust Catherine Auman and welcome her perspective."

— Vince Kelvin, Seminar Leader and Coach

Tantric Mating

Using Tantric Secrets to
Create a Relationship
Full of Sex, Love and Romance

Catherine Auman, LMFT

Green Tara Press

Green Tara Press

Los Angeles, CA

www.greentarapress.com

"The #1 Thing You Can Do to Improve Your Relationships" and "The Quickest Route to Tantric Sex" were previously published in Catherine Auman's book *Shortcuts to Mindfulness: 100 Ways to Personal and Spiritual Growth.*

The Atisha Heart Meditation is an abbreviated version of that found on osho.com

Library of Congress Control Number: 2021924359

Library of Congress In-Publication Data

Auman, Catherine I.

Tantric Mating: Using Tantric Secrets to Create a Relationship Full of Sex, Love and Romance

1. Self Help 2. Dating 3. Spiritual

ISBN: 978-1-945085-18-5 Paperback

ISBN: 978-1-945085-19-2 Electronic Book Text

Author Photo by Charity Burnett

About the Author photo by Stephanie Westfall

Front cover art by Anna Heimkreiter

Cover and interior design by Lilly Penhall

CONTENTS

INTRODUCTION

When I met my Perfect Beloved, it looked and felt like magic. We had each been attending a tantra workshop that taught massage techniques and after a few sessions, he asked me to partner with him. What followed, we like to say, was "love at first touch." After a couple of months dating, we decided to be exclusive, then after two years, we got married. We are both always saying, "I didn't know it could be this good."

It seemed like magic when we met because that is what we've been led to believe by movies, fairy tales, Disney princesses and superheroes. It looked and felt like magic because when we met, we both experienced something beyond what we'd ever felt before. Our coming together even seemed like something of the divine. And yet, it wasn't magic because we created it, by preparing ourselves by the inner and outer work we'd each been doing in a dedicated manner for a very long time.

We'd both been on personal and spiritual growth paths for decades. Both of us had received years of therapy and coaching to heal our childhood traumas. Greg had been helped by psychedelics used in a healing capacity. I'd been studying tantra both individually and in groups most of my adult life. For both of us, our personal and spiritual growth was the most important thing in our lives, and in this way, our frequencies matched perfectly.

Osho, the great tantra master, once said, "Tantra is the science of transforming ordinary lovers into soulmates. And that is the grandeur of Tantra. It can transform the whole earth; it can transform each couple into soulmates." I love this quote because it lets us know there is something we can do, that love is not some accident or luck, but that by learning and practicing tantric principles, any serious student of love can create a soulmate relationship like the one Greg and I have.

When you are both on dedicated personal and spiritual growth paths, when you are safe to talk about everything, when the sex is jaw-droppingly exquisite every single time, when you just plain love hanging out together as friends—isn't that what we're all looking for? In this book and the others in the series, I show you how to attract and relish this caliber of a relationship.

There are two parts to *Tantric Mating*: the part you do on yourself before you meet your partner and continue after you find them, and the work you do as a couple. Much of what you can do alone is taught in my book *Tantric Dating: Bringing Love and Awareness to the Dating Process*, which is about turning yourself into a more loving person. I had to do a lot of work on myself to attract love, because as the half-loving person I found myself to be, I could only attract half-loving partners. I wanted more than that and was willing to work for it.

Tantric Mating: Using Tantric Secrets to Create a Relationship Full of Sex, Love and Romance continues the teaching about how to become half of a perfect partnership whether you're single or partnered. Personal and spiritual growth are ongoing, and people who are fully alive are engaged in the process until their last breath. I don't believe we ever come to the endpoint of becoming as fully loving as we can be—but if that completion is possible, it's a goal worth pursuing.

Then there's the part you do together. When Greg and I fell in love, we had to decide what kind of relationship we wanted to create as a couple. Both of us had been in relationships in the past that were painful, and we didn't want to repeat those mistakes. We also had to confront misinformation from the mainstream culture. We found that our intimacy and sex life were enhanced by our best friend status, not diminished.

We found that sex, when there are no resentments lingering between us as a couple, is way beyond conventional expectations. Since the space between us was completely clear, because we had worked on ourselves and carried no resentments, because we had exercised our bodies and kept them healthy and relaxed, even though we were at an age when sex is supposed to have gone downhill, we found ourselves more sexual and more sexually satisfied than ever before. It was shocking and amazing that sex could be this good, even "psychedelic." Nothing we'd heard of before led us to expect this.

In *Tantric Dating*, the secrets of why you haven't found love and how to find it are explained. The third book in the series, *Tantric Relating*, is about how you can communicate both verbally and non- to keep the love fires burning. In this book, *Tantric Mating*, you'll learn how to be in partnership and create your perfect soulmate relationship. You'll find out how soulmates are created and that they do not come to us by magic, how conventional advice has steered us wrong, what kind of work to do on yourself, that tantric sex really is as good as they say, and how to live in a perpetual honeymoon.

And so, I want to teach you my method of *Tantric Mating* that created the soulmate relationship I had dreamed of since childhood, after I found my Perfect Beloved using my *Tantric Dating* method. This book can change your life, your love, and your partner, if they are willing. You must be available to hear truth that is outside the conventional world of advice, for that is not where truth resides. It's up to you to create the soulmate relationship of your dreams. It is within your reach, if only you will reach far enough. When you become the loving person you truly are, love is ever-present.

TANTRIC MATING MINDSET

Soulmates Are Created, Romance Is Created

Millions sit waiting passively for a love that never arrives. Both men and women lie like Sleeping Beauty, hoping they will be kissed and woken up. We dream of a love that enlivens, raises us to an exalted level of being, just like that portrayed in movies, books, songs, and fairy tales. The magical lover will arrive, the Perfect Beloved, the one with whom we will become complete. Finally.

We've been taught to passively wait, and to focus on exteriors. Previously women, but now men in equal numbers as social media has changed the game, spend anxious hours fretting about their appearance and doing whatever they can to improve it. Previously men, but now women in equal numbers, focus on the money it will take to make themselves love-worthy: clothes, cars, cosmetics, cosmetic procedures. We go to the gym, improve our nutrition, learn sex skills online, adopt attitudes from rap, and engage in hookups while we wait.

The beginning of most relationships dangles the promise that the dream romance has finally appeared. Its wonder descends and for a while, from three months to two years, we're entranced. If we're lucky enough to be in a relationship that lasts that long, often we don't know how to keep it, so we move on, hoping to magically find the dream with someone else. As you know, our relationship break-up rate is now well over 50 percent. That is a lot of heartbreak.

Many of us feel hopeless. I know I certainly felt hopeless before I figured it out. Usually the questions asked are, "Where can I meet men/women? Where is she/he?" We are hoping to be at the right place at the right moment where we will meet (without any effort on our part) and mutually fall in love at first sight, what Hollywood terms the "cute meet." You've seen this moment in numerous rom-coms: the future lovers don't even like each other at first, in fact, they are irritated by each other, but since it was fated and otherworldly all along, they fall in love and live happily ever more.

The problem with these scenarios and the sitting around waiting is that love is not passive at all. You'll never find the love your heart is longing for unless you're willing to work for it. Love and romance are something we create, and no artist of any art form expects to achieve a masterpiece without putting in the effort, discipline, work, mistakes, and steady improvement it takes to get good at anything. No one arrived one night starring at the Hollywood Bowl by sitting and wishing for it to happen. No one has become successful in their career by waiting for a "cute meet."

The fact of the matter is that if you want the sex, love and romance you've always dreamed of, you're going to have to be the one to create it. It's not coming from the sky. You'll have to make it happen. The right question is, "What do I need to do and be to attract and create my perfect love?"

Conventional Expectations

When Greg and I decided to get married, we chose a cute little chapel downtown. We were planning a big party later in the year for friends and family, but for now, we didn't want to wait to make our commitment. We got all dressed up, arrived at our appointed time, and the first order of business was to fill out the paperwork. The woman in charge, who also turned out to be the person who would marry us, within a few minutes asked Greg a question to which he answered, "Yes." Much to our surprise, she responded, "Now that you're getting married, that's how it's going to be from now on: 'Yes, ma'am. No, ma'am.'" We thought maybe she was trying to be amusing but from the look on her face, it didn't appear so.

It continued the whole time we were there. At one point, the woman pointed out that once we were married, "She's the boss." During our ceremony, she noticed I didn't have any flowers and she chided Greg for not getting me any, giving him a mini-lecture on "You have to get her roses, and not just on Valentine's Day."

None of these conventional ideas apply to us whatsoever. Greg knows that if I want flowers, I will buy them. He expresses his romantic feelings frequently in a way that fits for him and for me, and neither of us is "the boss." It was really weird to have these conventional expectations about love and marriage show up in so tender a moment that was supposed to be about us.

Around the same time, we had a guy remodeling our home, and Greg was supervising. I don't usually care too much about the details in the house, except for certain things. Greg pointed out to the guy that he had fitted a tile wrong, and he responded, "Oh, she's not going to like that." Greg explained that I really don't care about stuff like that. The next day when the handyman showed up for work, the first thing he said to Greg was, "Was she mad about the tile? Did you get in trouble? You know how women are."

Where is this all coming from? Conventional expectations. For many people, this is the story they have in their heads when they interact.

If you turn on the television for a few hours, there are constant messages and images about all kinds of ideas that may or may not be true. There are jokes and storylines about the supposed "war" between men and women. We are constantly told that men are inconsiderate slobs who only want sex, not intimacy or affection. Women rarely want sex; just leave them alone. Your life is basically over once you're in a committed relationship, and if you get married, you're never having sex again. Once married, you don't want to see each other and all you're going to do is fight. All of these messages and images create a mindset and behavior that have been normalized by mainstream culture so much so that we often think they're true without even questioning them.

One of the first things we want to do is to identify what conventional expectations about sex, love and romance we have adopted from the mainstream culture that may not be true and challenge them.

The Work You Do on Your Own

Whether you are single or partnered, you'll need to work on yourself to create Tantric Mating, but not in the way you think. We've been told many untruths, such as it's all about improving our appearance, or being more youthful or slim, or owning more stuff, but that's not how you find or create love. Love is a question of frequency, and the higher yours is, the higher the frequency of the relationship you'll be able to attract and create.

Ways to raise our frequency can be thought of holistically in different arenas: the physical, emotional, financial, and spiritual. Physically, you'll want a fit and lively body to make love, go on walks together, give and receive massages, and enjoy the activities of daily life until well past the age when most people expect to be old. That means you'll need to clean up your food and exercise. If you want more than average results, you'll have to pay more than average attention.

Then we must consider how you feel about your body. You won't be able to have great sex if you haven't learned to love your own shape and discarded any nonsense from the culture that bodies aren't beautiful the way they are. Stop following social media that promotes body shaming, ageism, and materialism; instead, choose to follow those that promote loving values.

Raising the frequency of our emotional life involves dealing with any baggage from the past, so clean that stuff up. If you had a difficult childhood and thus difficult relationships afterward, you'll most likely benefit from therapy.

Here are some questions to ask yourself to assess your emotional maturity: Are you an independent, non-codependent adult? Are you able to soothe your own feelings of loneliness, fear, doubt, insecurity? Are you emotionally reactive, meaning, when you get mad, do you yell, break things, throw tantrums? Are you disrespectful toward others? If you don't want these things in your love life, best to make sure they are weeded out of yourself.

Are you financially stable? It's not necessary to be wealthy or have a lot of money, but it is important to be able to pay your bills and have little to no debt. If you are not covering the basics and haven't put anything away for a rainy day, it will show up in feelings of insecurity and low self-esteem. To attract stable love, make sure your own life is stable.

If you want someone who is ready to make a full commitment, ask yourself if you have made a full commitment to your career, a pet, your own life? If you're unsure, in flux, or waiting to find a partner before making important decisions, you'll attract a person who's unsure about you whether you are single or partnered.

The best thing you can do to attract and maintain love is to make sure that you are a loving person. If you are only a halfway-loving person, you will attract a person who is only half-loving. Ask yourself, "Am I soulmate material?" and if there are areas listed above that need attention, do your work until the answer is yes. You don't need to be perfect, but if you dream of perfect love, or as we are calling it Tantric Mating, you are half of that equation.

Friendship Is Required for Tantric Sex

Word on the street is that "the friend zone" is the dead end of romantic possibility and certainly not where you'll find great sex. That may be true if what you're seeking is a wild weekend with a fantasy figure, which often includes, if you've bought into conventional daydreams, the delicious pain of being rejected afterward. If this type of rainbow beginning ever does "work out," you will always be wondering if your partner really loves you or if it's a relationship based on appearances because deep trust has not been established.

Dr. John Gottman, a psychologist in Seattle and big kahuna relationship guru, has been conducting research in his "Love Lab" for decades on what makes relationships work. He observed and measured couples with the aid of electrodes as they got along, argued, had fun. His wife, Dr. Judy Gottman, a practicing psychotherapist, put his research results into action with her clients, and together they have developed trainings for therapists and written best-selling books.

One of the most jaw-dropping findings of the Gottmans is that 69 percent of people in successful partnerships rate the friendship as the most important element. When I first heard this, I was stunned. I had been brainwashed to believe that men would rate sex as by far the most important thing, but the majority do not.

If friendship is the most important component of a successful relationship, why have we not been emphasizing it? Encouraging it? Helping people enhance it? Why are singles being told to avoid being "in the friend zone" at all costs? Someone who is our best friend is exactly who we should be looking for and what we should be growing in our partnerships.

If you want to be really relaxed in bed, if you want to feel free to be creative, if you want to know you will not be shamed, that your good qualities will be appreciated and your not-so overlooked, if you want to snuggle and hug and not be judged on your performance, and to know with absolute certainty that your lover will not leave you if you gain five pounds, you'll need to cultivate the quality of best-friendship with your lover.

To relax enough into the mystery for tantric sex to occur, you'll need to build total trust. You both need to know that anything that happens will be okay, that you are not being judged but rather honored and held, and that anything that comes up is welcome.

This applies if you are single as well. You can be friends and friendly with a one-night stand, a short-term relationship or a long one. That quality of friendliness comes from you. You care about sharing, honoring, and having fun. Not some heavy breathing, pain-filled horror show of people using one other to enhance their egos.

Osho said, "Friendship is higher than love." In the year that I lived at the tantra ashram, friendship always came first. Friendship doesn't diminish sexuality; it enhances sexuality. Many people say they don't agree, but when I ask them, "Have you ever had really intimate sex?" they invariably answer that, no, they have not. For soul-stirring, heart-centered, really intimate tantric sex, friendship is a prerequisite.

Safety Is the Root of Everything

All extraordinary relationships and phenomenal sex are based on a foundation of safety. In tantra, we say that this stems from the root or the base chakra, down close to your tailbone. This safety is the root of the tree of your relationship with others and the world. There are three areas to consider: your own safety, your partner's, and the safety of the relationship.

First, when considering your own safety, do you feel safe in the world? If your childhood was not a safe place, you may grow up feeling insecure. If you experienced sexual molestation or assault, more likely than not, you won't find sex to be safe. You may have been taught not to trust men or women or gender-fluid people. To heal these issues, revisiting them in psychotherapy may help.

You may not feel safe if you are not in the best physical health, or because you fear aging and losing your attractiveness. (We don't lose our attractiveness with age unless we believe we do, but that's for another book.)

Another facet of considering our own safety is, are you safe for other people? Is another person safe with you? Can they be sure you will not diss them behind their back? Are you the kind of person who is there when needed, or are you a fair-weather friend? Can your partner trust you to speak your truth? Are you hiding something that if your partner found out, they would be hurt?

Secondly, consider if your partner, or the person you are considering for a partner, is a safe person. This may take some time to deduce. Certainly, you want to make sure they are not physically or sexually abusive, but also not emotionally unkind, meaning you can trust they will not make fun of you, deride or shame you, or be overly sensitive or reactive.

Building a safe relationship means that when together, you are able to be your true selves. It means that when you are ready for intimacy, you have created a safe space free from interruption. It means making agreements so that you know what to expect, and that the two of you are on the same page.

New lovers need to take time to learn to feel safe with each other. However, even couples who have been together for twenty-five years may find that they don't trust each other right now. Trust and safety are works in progress, and their maintenance is ongoing.

In a previous relationship, I didn't feel safe with my partner because I suspected he was flirting with other women over text and social media. Because of that, I decided early on in my relationship with Greg that I didn't want that for us. I let him know that there was nothing I had to hide, there would be no one I would be flirting with, and that he had full access to my phone or email if he wanted to check. I also decided to always report to him whenever some guy doesn't realize I'm married and flirts with me. I don't have to do this, but I want Greg to feel absolutely safe and secure. Greg has never asked to see my phone or email—he doesn't have to, and I don't have to look at his either. This is just one of our practices that has established complete safety with each other.

Safety is needed to be able to fully relax in one another's presence. Relaxation is the key to intimacy and great sex.

Soulmate Creation and the Centers

Osho said that soulmate creation has to do with the centers being aligned. First, we'll take a look at what the centers are, and then in the next chapter, how to get them into alignment. Tantra uses the word "chakras," but many people are uncomfortable with Sanskrit terms, so we'll use the word "centers" instead.

There are seven centers in the body, placed along the spine, starting at the tailbone. These centers are not actual physical entities, although they do seem to line up with the glands of the endocrine system. People of higher vision and wisdom have seen them as spinning centers of energy. When they are whirling freely, each energy center can be experienced as free and unblocked. Everyone differs in the level of development in each of their centers, and in their level of development compared with others.

1)   We previously talked about how the root or base center is concerned with safety, the safety required for all trusting relationships and for tantric sex. The first center is about security, vitality, and whether we feel good about being alive. A person who has moved around a lot might not feel safe and secure, or someone who's experienced trauma may have challenges establishing a sense of rootedness, connectedness, and commitment to life.

2)   The second center is located around the genitals and is about sexuality and emotions. (Anybody notice that emotions and sex are often connected?) It is just about impossible to grow up in this culture and not have unresolved issues about sex. Most couples are unmatched in terms of how often they want sex, what kind, and differences in each person's past experience.

3)   The third center resides in the belly and is about power, personal and otherwise. One reason we've had trouble in our relationships is because of the power struggles going on. I was taught in graduate school that the power

struggle stage lasts for the first twenty-three years of the relationship. I don't know if that's true or not, as I've never been in a relationship of that length, but I do know that it's possible to avoid power struggles if each person has developed their own sense of personal power. If you look out in the world, a lot of power struggles are going on all over the planet.

4)   Some people think that the world as a whole is trying to wake up in the fourth center, the heart center. You can really notice the difference between people whose heart centers are beginning to open, those who are living from the heart, wanting to spread love, and those who haven't gotten there yet. We've all got a long way to go to blossom fully into love.

5)   The fifth center is in the throat and is about truth speaking. Most of us have large blocks in this center from trying not to speak our truth from fear of being misunderstood or because it's not going to be politically correct. We may not speak because we know the corporate world doesn't want to hear what we have to say. Many of us have been outsiders, so

we have kept quiet about our beliefs and opinions. Many relationship "experts" (not me) teach that there are things you're supposed to say and things you shouldn't so people will be attracted to you. We've all grown up with that idea since high school.

6)   The sixth center is in the middle of the forehead and is about true seeing, vision and philosophy. As it's rare for relationships to be hampered by this and the next center, we won't be spending much time on them.

7)   The seventh center at the top of our head relates to our sense of spirituality and connection to the divine.

Take the time right now to assess where you are. The more we work on ourselves and the areas of our lives that these centers represent, the freer and more energetic we become.

The higher you are in your development, the higher the frequency of the partner you will attract and the greater your chances of creating the soulmate relationship of your dreams. Where are you in the development of your centers?

Soulmates' Centers Are Aligned

In soulmate relationships, the centers are aligned, meaning, the development of each center in one person is mirrored back by the partner's. Ideally, we would have an individual with perfect flowering in every center meeting another perfect person, but of course that never happens. Each of us is more advanced in one center than another, and we all have room to grow. What you can do is to work individually on evolving your own centers, and when in a relationship, work together to strengthen and bring yourselves into alignment. The more areas you match up, the more likely the relationship has soulmate potential.

The problems in relationships can be described as misalignments in these centers. An example is that two people meet and one person has a more developed heart center and wants a heart connection, while the other person's sex center is developed but not their heart. Another example is that many couples get stuck with underdeveloped power centers and so are madly trying to be one-up all the time, and find they are not able to speak truth to one another.

Center imbalances can show up in other ways. For example, a lot of so-called spiritual people are in what we call spiritual bypass. Their upper centers are open: They are very spiritual, praying and meditating, fasting, worrying about maintaining a pure vegan diet and so forth, but they don't have a job or are unkind to others. They need to work on maturing their lower centers so that they have a good solid foundation to support a relationship.

The first thing to do is to assess where you are with your center development. The second is to work on boosting them, because the more advanced the centers, the happier you will be, and the closer you will be to soulmate creation. Here are some suggestions:

1.   First Center (Safety): Wake up your body and your aliveness, practice Osho Kundalini Meditation, beautify your home, ask yourself

frequently, "Am I in my body? Am I safe?" take steps to establish ongoing safety for yourself and others, shake your booty and stamp your feet.

2.   Second Center (Sex and Emotions): Learn sexual skills, basic through advanced, deprogram yourself from conventional sexual conditioning, clear past trauma with a therapist, overcome cultural shaming, live life sex-positively.

3.   Third Center (Power): Take 100 percent responsibility for your results and your life, get yourself to a place where you can say, "My life works," become financially stable.

4.   Fourth Center (Heart): Adopt a pet, learn to be universally social, donate time and/or money to a charity that inspires you, practice kindheartedness, repair things with your family.

5.   Fifth Center (Truth Speaking): Learn to speak with authenticity; join groups where genuine speaking is encouraged and supported, for example, Twelve-Step groups or group therapy; make agreements with your partner

about how much truth you want to share in your relationships.

Begin with maximizing the first five centers. Without the development of these areas, the relationship will not have strong enough legs to support it. After that, you can focus on expanding the higher centers: intuition, true seeing, and spirituality.

Working on your centers takes place both individually and as a couple. If you are single, the more your centers are strengthened, the higher the frequency of a partner you will attract. And when you are in a relationship, use this guide to raise your partnership to the elevation of soulmates.

Orgasm Is Not What You Think

Orgasm is not what you think. We've been brainwashed by the conventional culture to believe that orgasm is something it's not. This indoctrination is so pervasive we don't even question the notion that orgasm is the goal of sex. It's part of what it is, but that's not the whole understanding.

We've been taught that the point of sexual play with another being is to stimulate each other with increasing intensity to the point of orgasm. Conventional sex goes like this: foreplay, she comes, he comes, it's over. For non-hetero couples, negotiation is required, but the blueprint remains the same. This is, of course, better than historical sex where the female's pleasure was disregarded, but this pattern we're supposed to perform gets very boring. We've even been provided with bar graphs to show us how our arousal should go up, up, up, and then drop off, as if this is optimal.

In this type of sex, every movement is geared toward the eventual orgasm. Everything is leading up to it with tension and strain. The more intense it is, the better. Women are expected to come every time like men do, and if they don't, everyone is grumpy. The idea is that orgasm is something to strive for, that it takes effort, and we often find ourselves disappointed, again. It becomes a performance marker for how good the sex is.

This style of sex has been the mainstream model since the 1970s when it was deified by Masters and Johnson. Yes, there have always been people who enjoyed this type of sex, but it was not always considered the end-all and be-all. Masters and Johnson began studying arousal in laboratories, measuring it, and so forth. Thus began the conventional codification of lovemaking—that it should look like this, act like that, and take this particular path to completion. I don't think laboratory sex knows anything about the essence of sex, and this research has created a complete misunderstanding of sexuality.

Something more profound has been going on since the beginning of time—what we call *tantra*. Let me share with you how I discovered this. Soon after I arrived in India at the tantra ashram where I was to live for a year, I was lying relaxing on my bed. My breath began to deepen and circle in a loop from my nostrils to my tailbone with no beginning or end. Without any intention, a part of me surrendered, and the breathing started happening by itself. Orgasmic waves rushed through my body... pulsating—it was so enjoyable.

Days later, I went to an event called Energy Darshan. Music was playing, and everyone was dancing vigorously. All of a sudden, completely unexpectedly, an energy shot up my spine and my vagina began contracting. I realized, oh my God, I'm having an orgasm! How could this be? I was having an energy orgasm just from dancing, not from a partner or from touching myself.

Over the course of that year, there were several times when unexpected orgasms would bless me. In *Tantric Dating*, I recounted an incident at the Burning Ghats when out of the blue, an orgasm rushed up my spine, and I felt overwhelming joy. I had hitched a ride on the orgasm wave.

Orgasm is actually a pulsating frequency that is always going on in the universe, buzzing and humming underneath everything. It is a level of bliss that never stops. When we engage in conventional sex where we struggle, get to the orgasm, and poof! it's gone—we have come up and met this frequency briefly.

When you choose not to have conventional sex and instead practice tantra, you can learn to catch a ride on the orgasm wave, and then it doesn't stop. It can last for minutes or hours or days. It depends on your level of development, your relaxation, and your capacity for bliss. It's possible to lift your own frequency by the practice of tantric exercises, certain ways of making love, particular ways of breathing, and then you can surf along this vibrating frequency. You catch it. You ride it. You know if you let go, you can always catch a wave again.

This is what orgasm is. This knowledge has been withheld from you by people who don't have a clue. I want you to experience this level of orgasm because once you do, you will want it in your life. There's no doubt about that.

Sacred Sexuality

In tantra, sex is sacred, as is the body. This is a radically different attitude than the one most of us grew up with. The majority of us learned that sex is naughty and that pleasure is something we need to sneak. The conventional worldview of the last two thousand years has been that the body is sinful; thus sex and pleasure are too. We've learned to live ignoring our bodies, which encourages people to walk around as merely heads—looking, thinking, analyzing, and judging—rather than feeling the wisdom that the body can bring.

One of the first tasks of Tantric Mating is to befriend your body and those of your lover(s) and honor them as sacred. When you do so, it's possible to gaze in amazement at their breathtaking beauty, their seemingly endless capacity for pleasure, and their innate wisdom. When you hold sex as sacred, you begin to honor your partner, your body and theirs, your sexual organs, your pleasure, and the space you make love in as manifestations of the divine.

As a tantric practice, you can remember to remember that you are embodied, that this moment is sacred, that this man or woman is my beloved in this moment, and that these sexual feelings are sacred. You can cultivate these attitudes within yourself and through practice become more open to love and to life. It's a discipline like any other, such as learning to play tennis or chess or how to speak French.

Osho once said that the best sex is had by meditators. Meditation is a practice of touching the sacred in daily life. I believe what Osho meant was that tantric people are practicing mindfulness while we have sex. Consciously, we're staying in the present moment, not trying to get somewhere in the future. We're not thinking about lunch, or the news, or the multiplication tables, which is what they teach men to do so they won't come so quickly. (Thanks, guys, for doing that, but we'd rather have your presence.) We're not trying to get to orgasm; we're too busy enjoying the present moment. Just to touch each other's hands mindfully is making love.

When you are fully embodied as you touch another's flesh, you can notice when you aren't present or when you are spacing out. As a practice, you can remind yourself to stay present as much as possible and bring that to lovemaking. Always you come back to the present moment with full awareness, just as we do in meditation.

By practicing mindful, sacred sex with your lover, you may share an experience of the divine. You may even participate in what might be called "psychedelic sex." It all depends on letting go of what the conventional culture has taught you about unloving, mechanical sex, and bringing heart, love, and mindfulness to lovemaking, plus a sense of worshipping your beloved as a god or goddess.

Sex Is a Conversation

Sex is a conversation, a wordless exchange. Everything between you and your partner and all things enveloping the two of you are there in the bedroom. Every aspect gets communicated: the level of your commitment, whether or not you are able to open in vulnerability and trust, your ability to hold or not hold each other's gaze, or if you can let go and let the bodies make love instead of the minds. Sex is a conversation between lovers about what they mean to each other. Every touch, stroke, heartbeat, endearment, and sigh conveys a message.

During sex, you are also communicating nonverbally about the difficulties in your relationship. Boredom, untruths, withholds, and conversations that have not been had will show up as "I'm not in the mood" or less-than-stellar lovemaking. Sometimes when making love brings you back into that state of being so close, looking into each other's eyes, intimate and safe, it transcends those problems. Sometimes it doesn't.

Men, it seems, often prefer to speak through the language of sex rather than through talking. Men express love through their penis, which is a beautiful thing about men. We've been brainwashed that this is something terrible—that men only want "one thing." It's quite beautiful, really, but in a sex-negative culture, we're not able to see that. Men want to express love sexually. They're looking to share it in the way that men convey love.

It's a tantric perspective that sex and love can be the same thing. But because of our cultural programming, we're not able to see that this is the way men are driven to love and connection. Neither men nor women have been taught this. Men want to share themselves. They want to express.

What if we interpreted men's desire for sexual connection as the hunger to connect, instead of, oh, he just wants sex? What if connection through sex is beautiful rather than a negative thing? A man wanting to have sex is often a bid for intimacy and love.

This is not meant to imply that if you just have sex, it will take care of all your problems. Sometimes when the conversation seems to be going nowhere, you can open yourself to the possibility that a beautiful conversation about your relationship can be had while you're making love.

Sex is a language we have that isn't verbal. It's a communication, a way to express love and to work out problems. It's a way to reconnect without having to do all this psychologizing. Much of the time, it's much more effective.

Psychedelic Sex

Tantric sex is as good as you've heard it is. It has little resemblance, however, to the conventional style of sex which consists of effort, tension, focus on the goal of orgasm, explosion and release, and when it's over, both parties are spent.

If sex is not about the goal of orgasm, what do you have? You have the sensual pleasure of being in this exquisite space with your lover, awareness of their touch, breath, and movement, the spiritual connection between you, and the promise of growing intimacy. You have the realization that this present moment is all there is. The partner is your beloved, your perfect love, your soulmate. Your being together is actually generating more love in the world, rather than the energy being discharged in the sex act. You have the opportunity to learn to sustain a state of pleasure and bliss for longer periods of time, instead of ending quickly because your nervous system hasn't yet learned to tolerate that much happiness.

Tantrikas (people who practice tantra) have told of altered states while having sex for hours that are similar to those brought about by psychedelic drugs. There are reports of sex being mind-shattering, life-changing, and reality-altering. People say they have felt an all-encompassing sense that this sexual union comes from a divine source, a perception of merging with their partner. Some people disclose that they've seen gods and goddesses in the bedroom, or energy and light. Some have talked about time traveling or remembering past lives, a sense of divine union, or experiencing ecstasies more powerful than orgasm. Tantric sex and psychedelics have in common being anchored in the present moment, experiencing altered states, and the possibilities for bliss, transcendence, and healing.

When you make love without the goal of orgasm, every touch to the skin is different—it has no intention other than to enjoy the moment. You can relax into protracted pleasuring of each other. When you have conventional sex, you will usually be finished in about twenty minutes or less. In tantric sex, if we want to cultivate "psychedelic" experiences without the use of psychedelic drugs, we have noticed the following timings:

- After 45 minutes, the mind falls silent

- After 2 hours, certain phenomena appear

- After 3 hours, a heightening of psychedelic phenomena

- After a certain amount of time, the bodies start making love by themselves

- 6–10 hours of lovemaking are possible, a whole weekend

Greg and I rarely decide to have an orgasm. Instead, we prefer to hitch a ride on the orgasmic waves that carry us blissfully along for who-knows-how-long.

Creating Magic

You know it's you, right? who's responsible for creating the magic in your relationship—not your partner, Tinkerbell, or the goddess of love. The good news is that there are so many ways to up the magic quotient and increase the likelihood of living happily ever after. Here are some tantric suggestions:

- First of all, choose a partner you can trust. Whether you've been together for years or have recently met, you'll need to share deep trust with your partner in order to create magic. If there are conversations you need to have to reestablish trust, schedule them now. If this seems daunting, hire a competent marriage and family therapist to help.

- Clear your relationship. Anything still nagging you from the past with your partner, whether it was this morning or months ago, will keep the magic from happening. It will also show up in the bedroom. These are conversations that need to be had, and keep being had, so that your relationship stays clear from unspoken resentment and unhappiness. (This is covered in detail in my book, *Tantric Relating*.)

- Cultivate an attitude of gratitude and devotion to your partner. Become thankful that this partner chooses to be with you, and express it frequently. Choose to focus on your partner's divinity rather than, like most people, their flaws.

- Make plenty of time. A relationship takes time: time to hang out, time to plan, time to make love. Many people today need to prioritize their relationship and schedule time together and make dates.

- Make a sacred space. The bedroom is a good place to start as this is where you make love. Do you have beautiful linens that feel good to your skin? Plump, comfy pillows? Art on the walls that reflects an environment of beauty and sensuality? Create a magic bedroom devoid of anything other than that which promotes sleep or lovemaking.

- When you touch, focus awareness inside your own body, or where your partner is touching. Notice, as you would while meditating, when your attention is in the past or the future, and gently bring it back to the present moment with your partner. That mindfulness brings gentle magic to being together and to touch.

- Create playlists of music that is intoxicating to make love to. It is usually recommended to use music without words, or words in a foreign language so you're not distracted. For tantric sex, music that is calming and meditative is preferred so as to stay slow and relaxed. Most conventional "sexy music" encourages tension and release. Experiment and find out what is best for you.

- Be in your body, not your head. Magic occurs when we drop down into our bodies and leave thinking behind. Mental chatter can easily destroy connecting.

- Drop the idea of "foreplay." In tantra, we give up the idea that how we pleasure ourselves before intercourse is somehow less important. We find all actions of lovemaking equally pleasurable and sacred, and we may not even do these things "before." Tantrikas don't feel the need to follow the conventional formula for sex.

- Enjoy protracted pleasuring. Increase your ability to enjoy giving and receiving touch for its own sake, and not as an avenue for getting somewhere else (orgasm). This ability is a muscle that can be gotten into shape, and the practice is more fun than the gym.

- Go with whatever arises. Learn to relax and be with what is, rather than what conventional sex says you ought to be doing.

- Praise. Tell your partner when they look hot, or do a kind thing, or turn you on. Tell them frequently. Look for excuses to praise them. I've never heard of anyone saying, "Please! Stop telling me good things about myself!"

- "My only intention is to be fully present." Rather than being goal-oriented to sometime in the future, or trying to make something happen, tantra suggests we only intend to be fully present in the now.

- Practice eye gazing. When you look deeply into another person's eyes, it is impossible not to fall in love with them. Perhaps this is why we are afraid to do it. When I was in India at the tantra ashram, we did exercises where we looked into each other's eyes for twenty minutes, and we all couldn't stop crying—we fell in love with everyone in the room no matter what they looked like or who they were. This is perhaps a clue for how to create more magic and love in our partnerships and in the world.

Building and Maintaining Your Soulmate Status

"And they lived happily ever after." That little phrase from our favorite fairy tales sets us up for disappointment when our relationships don't glide on magically without effort on our parts. It's not exactly like that, is it? Instead, when we hear it's going to take work to maintain our relationships, that sounds like it's going to be difficult and treacherous. It may be if that's how you set it up, or it can be fun, sexy, and delightful.

First off, it requires maintaining the high frequency state you were in to be able to attract this great partner. That means continuing to attend to your physical health, your vitality, and your emotional stability, so that you're not flying off the handle about every little thing. It means staying interested in your life, being invested in something greater than yourself, such as your career or volunteer work. You must have passion for life to have a passionate relationship.

Secondly, it takes using and expanding your communication skills. This is so essential that the third book in the series, *Tantric Relating*, will go into it deeply, but for now, let's just say that every little challenge that gets swept under the carpet and not discussed will show up in the bedroom as "I'm not in the mood" or resentment against your partner. This leads to the conventional wisdom that it's inevitable that sex will decrease after the first two years of being together. But it is possible for you to nurture a really exciting sex life, and that's going to take attention as it doesn't happen just by itself.

Thirdly, you need to make time. Our lives are so busy, and if we don't prioritize intimate relations, they won't happen. If you'd rather just watch Netflix in the evening because it's easier, that's what your relationship will turn into. It's not a bad choice if that's what you want. But if your heart's desire is for a soulmate relationship with intimate, evolving sexuality, then that's going to require dedicated time.

Fourth, it's important to set goals for your relationship. What do you want to do together? What are your priorities? Travel, or would you rather design an oasis in the backyard? What are you up to as a couple?

Every year I make my personal goals, and then get together with Greg to make goals for our relationship. Last year we took up qigong and trained for a half-marathon. What do you want to do this year? Is there something you want to study together?

So again, there are the two aspects of maintaining your soulmate status: your own personal growth as well as your growth as a couple. What are you doing to maintain your half of the couple? And what are you doing together to cultivate and grow that? It is a project, if you want to look at it that way, a project of creating the soulmate relationship you've always dreamed of. Everyone's dreaming of it, but guess what? You make it happen.

A Perpetual
Honeymoon

Consider for a moment the word "honeymoon." You will discover a subtle brainwashing that says the beginning of a relationship is romantic and blissful, and the rest of it is not. The message is that you're going to be high on sexual attraction and love for a short period of time, and after that, it tanks. The very word "honeymoon" sets up an expectation that relationships inevitably go downhill.

This expectation of decline may dovetail with seeing your parents not having the soulmate relationship you dream of. Many of us grew up with people who fought a lot, some to the point of splintering the family by getting divorced. Other parents were asleep to each other, seemingly half-dead or on automatic pilot, which happens when there's a lot that's unspoken. Many people have never witnessed juicy, alive, long-term relationships, so they don't know it's possible. I've even had people ask me, "Do happy couples exist?"

Emphatically, yes. The higher possibilities were first shown to me years ago when I attended a party in Beverly Glen, an affluent neighborhood in the hills above Los Angeles. I was excited as I walked in because the gathering was for single people pursuing personal and spiritual growth. As always back then, I was searching for my true love and thought I might find him there. Instead of meeting him that night, what I experienced is still inspiring me today. Sitting and glowing with an unearthly radiance was an older couple, surprisingly sexy and hot. I had never seen any two people, let alone any one, so alive and full of energy! It was as if they were in the foreground and everyone else, backstage.

At that time, I still believed in the conventional ageism that older people aren't interested in sex. These two appeared to be on their honeymoon even though they had been together for years. I had to know what they knew and wanted to have what they had, so I went up and introduced myself. They knew secrets for sure—they were *tantrikas*, people who practice tantra. Seeing and being around their heightened energy was part of what set me out on my own journey of studying tantra and creating my perfect soulmate relationship. I ended up living in their house and learning from them, but that's for another book.

It was enlivening just to be in their presence. That's what a soulmate relationship can do—bring inspiration and more aliveness to those around them. From meeting this high-frequency couple, I knew sex and relationships could get better with age. Now, my husband and I are that couple.

You have the power to create your relationship to be a honeymoon that lasts, or you can slide into the aftermath that follows the conventional honeymoon. It really depends on what you and your partner want to create. If you want to have a wild, sexual, romantic ride, you can create that. If you don't mind that the romance and the sexuality decline with age and longevity, you can create that too. It's completely up to you. There's not some nebulous thing called a relationship that's out of your control, that's going to do what it wants. It's up to you and your partner.

By the way, how did you create your honeymoon if you had one? Or if you haven't, how do you imagine you would?

- You spent time planning activities that would delight the both of you.

- You allocated money and time to make it fabulous.

- You were on your best behavior—kind, humorous, full of praise.

- You focused on what was best about your partner—their body, their generosity, their integrity—and left the criticism in the trash where it belongs.

- You went out of your way to perform little romantic gestures.

- You made the effort to look your best.

- You dedicated exclusive time and space to you, your lover, and your love life.

If you decide you're going to create a perpetual honeymoon, these actions might be a good place to start.

Dedicated to Personal and Spiritual Growth

You now have all you need to create and maintain a soulmate relationship using the mindset and methods of *Tantric Mating*. The question is, will you do it? You must live your life dedicated to personal and spiritual growth and support this in your partner. You'll need to understand that growth is sometimes painful and that going through rough spots is often a good sign that you are growing. If you are increasingly expanding in the seven centers, if you are practicing seeing the divine in your partner, if you are excited to explore new ways of sexuality, you will create your Perfect Beloved and your soulmate relationship.

Some of you have been on the personal and spiritual growth path for years, while some of you are entering it now. It's all good. You're going to want to dedicate yourself to this growth for the rest of your life. The opportunity for more never stops. Osho, famed tantra master, says we have until our last breath to continue to evolve.

We talked in *Tantric Dating* about how if you're single, you'll want to be working on yourself, your physical health, your emotional stability, your financial wealth, your judgmental-ness, becoming a heart-centered person, and cultivating a more spiritual attitude toward others. You'll need to reject the methods the mainstream culture teaches to look for a partner, open your heart, and engage in personal work.

In *Tantric Relating*, we'll talk more about how to communicate verbally and nonverbally to create and keep your soulmate relationship alive. As a couple, you might choose activities to share together that promote personal and spiritual growth. The two of you may take hikes together to get lost in the splendor of nature. You may want to study and master some area of knowledge together, maybe take a class or tantra workshop to learn more about how to relate intimately and sexually.

I know that since my partner and I are both committed to our personal and spiritual growth paths that our relationship can only get better over time. There's a raft of societal brainwashing that sex, love, and romance only get worse as you get older. If you're both dedicated to personal and spiritual growth, it can only improve as you solve life's problems and create your life exactly as you want it. That is possible for you and is your future if you choose it.

TANTRIC MATING EXERCISES

Exercise #1: Challenging the Conventional Mindset

To become a free human being, it's essential to examine conventional beliefs and expectations and discard those that don't fit the world you want to create. Take some time and think through these commonly held "truths," and consider if you want to keep believing them or throw them out. Write your preferred attitude in the space below. An example of an alternative mindset is offered for the first conventional teaching.

- Young people are more attractive than older people.

  » Example: Attractiveness is actually enhanced by age due to a person's increasing sense of wisdom, self-esteem, and life mastery.

- The definition of who is "attractive" should be defined by advertising and social media.

- I can't help who I'm attracted to—it's in my DNA.

- Conventionally good-looking people are better candidates for love.

- Men want sex; women want love.

- Friendship means the death of sexual attraction.

- Marriage means sex goes downhill.

- People get less interested in sex as they get older, and if they don't, it's kind of gross.

- A sign of true love is that your partner can read your mind and fulfill your wishes without you having to do or say anything.

- Soulmates happen magically—it's either a soulmate relationship or it's not, and there's nothing you can do about it.

- Men lose freedom in marriage ("the old ball and chain").

- One person becomes the boss in the relationship. If it's the woman, the man's masculinity is in question.

- There exists a war between the sexes.

- Traditional sex roles should be reverted to for relationships to work.

- Everyone else is having great, trouble-free sex.

- I can't find a soulmate because I am too … (short, fat, old, poor, smart …).

- It means men don't love their partners if they don't do traditional things such as buy roses.

- Relationships are hard.

- Love happens by magic, and the best thing you can do is wait passively for its arrival.

- It's my partner's responsibility to keep the love, sex, and romance going in the relationship.

EXERCISE #2: Are You Soulmate Material?

The following is a questionnaire I developed for a matchmaking firm. How do you score? Is someone dreaming of you as their Perfect Beloved?

Physical

Are you still wearing clothes from 5 to 10 years ago?

Are you wearing old-people clothes?

Do you have an up-to-date haircut?

Are you sexy?

Do you have some kind of exercise routine?

Emotional

Do you have unresolved issues from your childhood?

Are you clinging to a past love? Are you still in love with someone?

Do you feel like it's okay to take out your frustrations on other people?

Financial

Are you financially stable?

Do you realize that anyone you marry will be responsible for your debt?

Are you in financial integrity?

Mental

Are you keeping up on current events, cultural and political, at least enough to converse?

Have you read a book in the past year? The past month?

Social

Do you have enough friends?

Are you universally social?

Do you have an interesting life that someone would like to join? Or are you a couch potato?

Home

Would your dream lover feel comfortable in your home?

Is your bedroom sexy?

When was the last time you bought new sheets? A new bedspread?

Spiritual

When did you last feel awe at the beauty of the universe?

Have you handled any addictions you might have?

Do you make any financial contributions to causes that inspire you? Do any charity work?

EXERCISE #3: The #1 Thing You Can Do to Improve Your Relationships

Feeling unappreciated is one of the main reasons people give for why they leave jobs and relationships. That's why it's so refreshing to hear what someone else appreciates about us. How nice is it to think of an oasis where someone is noticing what we do right.

The number one thing you can do today to improve your relationships is to tell someone what you appreciate about them. Not just a compliment like, "You look nice today," although under the right circumstances, that's always good. The trick is to use the word "appreciate" because that's what people are starving for, being appreciated. It is actually better if you notice a small thing because it is unexpected, and the person gets to feel that you are noticing and approving of them.

Simple examples might be, "I appreciate that you took our son to the ball game." "I appreciate that you take time for yourself, which allows me to do the same." "I appreciate that you take out the garbage before you're asked."

Mark and Diane were seeing me for marriage counseling because they were fighting and criticizing each other bitterly. I asked Mark to change gears and tell his wife something he appreciated about her. Diane waited nervously while Mark struggled to identify something, as this was a new way for him to think. When he finally said, "I appreciate that you dress so well for work," she broke out into a huge smile that looked as if he had given her a dozen roses. She hadn't known Mark was even paying attention.

Give it a try. Let your significant other off the hook and tell him or her a small thing you appreciate. Call your mother and give her "an appreciation." Let your employee know that you appreciate that she is always on time. Everyone can use a dose. Give someone the gift of appreciation today and watch your relationships blossom.

EXERCISE #4: Raise Your Frequency by Working on Your Centers

You've learned that soulmates' centers are aligned, and that the quality of your relationship depends on the work you do on your own. Now is your chance to create your action plan, and raise your frequency to the level of the relationship you are seeking. On pages 38-40, circle the actions that need attention, add ideas of your own, and create and implement your plan. Be sure to have fun—growth is a lifelong journey to be enjoyed.

My Action Plan:

First Center (Safety, Physical Body)

Second Center (Sex and Emotions)

Third Center (Power)

Fourth Center (Heart)

Fifth Center (Truth Speaking)

EXERCISE #5: Atisha Heart Meditation

"You will be surprised if you do [this meditation]. The moment you take all the sufferings of the world inside you, they are no longer sufferings. The heart immediately transforms the energy. The heart is a transforming force: drink in misery, and it is transformed into blissfulness."

– Osho, *The Book of Wisdom*

Bringing your awareness to your body and breathing, feel yourself here and now. Then bring your awareness to your heart chakra, the energy center in the middle of your chest. If it helps you, place one or both of your hands on your heart center. Absorb each in-breath into the heart, pour each out-breath out from the heart.

Start with your own misery, feel it with as much intensity as possible: the hurt, the wounds, and the suffering in your whole life. Accept it and welcome it. Breathe in your own misery... absorb it into the heart. Let it be transformed there into joy, into bliss. Breathe out all the joy, the blissfulness, pour yourself into existence.

Now expand this process. Take the whole misery of all beings, unconditionally, friends, enemies, family, strangers. Accept and welcome it. Breathe in all the misery and hell ... absorb it into the heart. Let it be transformed there into joy, into bliss. Breathe out all the joy, the blissfulness, pour yourself into existence.

Now completely withdraw your attention from the world, from others, even from yourself. Enjoy being silent and still.

EXERCISE #6: The Quickest Route to Tantric Sex

Tantra is about making love into an art. If you thought of yourself as an artist of love, what would you create? If you were painting a picture of the most juicy, delicious, perfect afternoon with your beloved, composing a song, or sculpting a masterpiece, how would you honor them?

Tantric lovers take their time. They are not in a hurry. Tantra has everything to do with savoring the moment, and bringing awareness to every detail. Noticing what you've never noticed before. Did you ever consider that the inside of the elbow could be an erogenous zone? That you can turn on your partner by tickling the small of his or her back?

The quickest route to tantric sex is to slow down, waaaay down. Do everything you normally do, but twice or even three times slower than usual.

Think of your gratitude for this moment, for your lover, for being able to express your celebration through your hands. Each moment is precious and sacred if you only pay attention. Be meditative, intimate; prolong the act of love.

Sting once told reporters that he and his wife, Trudie, practiced tantric sex for up to four hours at a time. He later explained that this time frame included their flirtation, having dinner, getting undressed, and sexual play, all as a part of tantric lovemaking. In tantra, these activities are not seen as "foreplay," but rather as opportunities for aware-ness and sexual pleasure; they are not less than intercourse itself.

Even if you think you are bored with this partner, with their body, approach it as if you've never been with it before. Watch with your awareness how much you can learn about pleasing a body you thought you knew. Enjoy your lover responding in ways you've never experienced before. How could anyone ever not be in the mood if every time were exquisitely different, shimmering with awareness? In tantric lovemaking, the quickest route is the slowest.

Acknowledgments

Thanks to my readers: Sandra Sloss Giedeman, Margaret Drewry Walsh, Lilly Penhall, and Kimberly Grace.

Thanks to my dream-come-true, my husband, Greg Lawrence.

Thanks for all the heartbreaks and heartaches, mistakes and missteps, broken fantasies and shattered dreams that were required along the way. They were all worth it to get HERE.

About the Author

Catherine Auman, LMFT (Licensed Marriage and Family Therapist) is a spiritual psychotherapist and the Director of The Transpersonal Center. She has advanced training in traditional psychology as well as the wisdom traditions. Catherine lived for a year at the Osho ashram in India—a full-time immersion in tantra and meditation—and she has studied and practiced tantra, love, sex, intimacy, and seduction with numerous teachers. She lives in Los Angeles with her husband, Greg Lawrence, with whom she teaches tantra and relationship enhancement.

Create the Sex, Love and Romance of Your Dreams with *The Tantric Mastery Series*

Imagine yourself in a perfect soulmate relationship full of sex, love and romance. Open yourself to love and awareness.

These three beautiful books teach you how.

Catherine Auman's *Tantric Dating: Bringing Love and Awareness to the Dating Process* was named one of the **Best Dating Books of All Time by BookAuthority**. *Tantric Mating: Using Tantric Secrets to Create a Relationship Full of Sex, Love and Romance* followed up this success by teaching what to do next after attracting your perfect love to maintain the magic. *Tantric Relating: Relationship Advice to Find and Keep Sex, Love and Romance* is about how to communicate both verbally and non- to keep the love fires burning.

Buy Now online or at your favorite retailer

Print, Ebook, or Audiobook

Connect with Catherine Auman

Websites:	catherineauman.com
	thetranspersonalcenter.com
Facebook:	catherineauman/author
Instagram:	@catherineauman
Youtube:	catherineauman
Eventbrite:	thetranspersonalcenter
Email:	info@catherineauman.com

Works by Catherine Auman

Books

The Tantric Mastery Collection: The Complete Tantric Mastery Series 3-in-1 Compilation

The Tantric Mastery Series (also available in Spanish)

    Tantric Relating: Relationship Advice to Find and Keep Sex, Love and Romance

    Tantric Mating: Using Tantric Secrets to Create a Relationship Full of Sex, Love, and Romance

    Tantric Dating: Bringing Love and Awareness to the Dating Process

Mindful Dating: Bringing Loving Kindness to the Dating Process

Guide to Spiritual L.A.: The Irreverent, the Awake, and the True

Shortcuts to Mindfulness: 100 Ways to Personal and Spiritual Growth

Fill Your Practice with Managed Care

Workshops

Tantra: The Science of Creating Your Soulmate

Tantra: The Foundations of Conscious Touch

Tantric Secrets about Women

Tantric Secrets about Men

Tantra and the Psychedelics of Sex

MDMA and Couples: The Promise of Ecstasy

Audio Recordings

Tantric Embodiment Induction

Deeply Relaxed

Awareness Breathing

Made in the USA
Monee, IL
24 September 2024